To DEBORAH

LOTS OF LOVE

ED

xo x

chRisTmas 13

SLIM'S
HEALTHY
KITCHEN

CHOOSE
BALANCE

Slim's Healthy Kitchen

429-431 Lisburn Road, Belfast, BT9 7EY

Victoria Square, Belfast, BT1 4QG

28 Belmont Road, Belfast, BT4 2AA

www.slimskitchen.com

Published by Slim's Healthy Kitchen.

Photography:

Khara Pringle

Kirth Ferris (Page, 6)

CONTENTS

In loving memory of our friend Chris Rice

INTRODUCTION

I was the big guy in school. I can say now, hand on heart, I brought my P.E. gear to school with me once in the five years I attended secondary school and I'm not sure I even wore it. I had even less interest in P.E. than the other seven subjects I was supposed to study. I had and still have the attention span of a goldfish and if something doesn't stimulate my mind, I'll have no interest in it.

Living in Belfast I travelled for an hour to and from Ballynahinch, Co. Down everyday to St. Colmans High School. I didn't sit my 11+ exam and therefore my options for choosing which secondary school to go to were limited. Most mornings I had the luxury of a friend's dad driving the two of us to school instead of having to sit on a cold school bus with heavily condensed windows and a smell of stale smoke. This luxury however, is how I believe the bigger guy in me came about. Each morning we stopped at a filling station to get stuff for mid-morning break. I normally climbed into the back seat of the car loaded with a full breakfast soda – bacon, sausage and fried egg between deep fried soda bread smothered in brown sauce. Looking back it wasn't really a great start to the day.

School dinners priced at 90p were another story, (rising to £1.20 with inflation throughout my time there)! This bought me a "Daily Special" each day. For my 90p I had two sausages, beans and stack of chips with a tin of Coke.

Eat, sleep and repeat for five years.

Nobody loves school but I hadn't caught the academic bug by 5th year and wasn't eager to complete my GCSE's or stay on at school. Instead I found an interest in music & technology, curious as to how things worked. I left school and I followed in my father's footsteps and took a job with my older brother embarking in a career in the electronic security business installing intruder alarms and CCTV. I also worked weekends in a local hotel, The Wellington Park where I served my time in pretty much every department from working on the reception desk to a couple of stints in housekeeping. Working here I learnt a lot and where I crafted by current work ethic. Most people aged 18 were out adventuring into nightclubs. I was more interested in getting a room transformed in time for a wedding and trying to find teaspoons.

Back to the day job... after a few years I struggled working with family (yes, brother I'm looking at you) and decided a change of career was needed. I took a job with Cafe Paul Rankin in Belfast. It was here that I began to build on my knowledge of the catering industry and made some life long friends, some of who, as it happens I now work with everyday. I worked here for almost four years but changes in the company meant a change in career for me again and I started my own business in my previous trade of electronic security. I worked at it for a few years but my heart was still in the kitchen. The idea of opening a "shop" that I could go to and get food for whatever the level of my hunger post gym work out came about after a few years of training and trying countless diets, working long days of early mornings and late nights.

I had been, quite literally, building a picture in my head for many years of how the "shop" would look, smell and feel. Living on my own I covered every wall in my house with print outs, cut outs, pictures, menu clippings and quotes. I finally let a close friend inside my head (showed him my kitchen wall). That friend was Jim Conlon and it was quite simple from here on in. Jim said to me if I didn't open the "shop" he would. This started the wheels in motion and a year later I opened the doors to the very first Slim's Healthy Kitchen on Belfast's Lisburn Road. Taking a massive gamble and not knowing how the good people of Northern Ireland would receive an idea that was thought up in my kitchen as we're a fickle bunch. As I write this now, we currently operate four outlets in Belfast, feed seventy pro-rugby players six meals a day and employ over one hundred full and part-time staff...and now the first cookbook!

The dream is very much real.

Slim xo

INGREDIENTS

Every street corner has a junk food option, every petrol station or shop you enter sells a massive bar of chocolate for £1 and there lies countless opportunities to be a glutton.

Food is fuel and that is its sole purpose, right? Well, maybe many, many years ago. Now food has evolved into so much more. For most of us it is a part of modern day life and a lot of our lives from a young age evolve around food. It may start with your mum asking on your way out the door to school what you wanted for tea. I lived in a house where not one of us ate the same thing and there are seven of us in the family.

As a society we have high expectations of how food should be. It should be delicious and make us feel good and now more than ever we want it in a hurry. We are all guilty of eating with short-term goals in mind, opting for a quick fix of comfort foods and often sugary foods.

I am of the firm belief that life is like our diet. The ingredients we use in the restaurant and in this cookbook are about balance, a mix of fun, excitement, enjoyment, smiles, laughter and hard work. Lets face it we have all had a weep chopping onions at some point.

At Slim's Healthy Kitchen we aim to bring a fresh approach food, by quite simply making healthier food choices more accessible and more exciting. Not everything we sell in our restaurants is über healthy, raw or organic. It's not what we are about. What we are about is choices. Walk into any of our restaurants and find something to eat around most diet choices from grass-fed meats, gluten free, paleo and even slimming world. Build your menu to how it suits you. The idea is that your partner, best friend or granny can come to enjoy a meal in a social environment with you, instead of asking for an egg white omelet and being looked at as though you are the odd one out.

Where milk is mentioned in any of the recipes, choose a product that suits you. Almond and soya milk are popular alternatives to dairy. Almond is probably the most popular choice across all of our restaurants for shakes. Made from ground almonds, it is lower in calories than other milks (the unsweetened kind). It is also free of cholesterol, saturated fat and is naturally lactose free. Soya milk made from soybeans is another popular milk alternative for vegans; it is naturally free of cholesterol, low in saturated fat and contains no lactose.

A balanced diet of fresh fruit and vegetables and meats from your local butcher or market is all you really need. There is not one fit all solution. It is about what works for you and what doesn't. We all have a friend that has pizza twice a week, doesn't go to the gym and still looks great in a bikini… if that's you then that's great but if you're like me, keep reading.

Throughout this cookbook you'll notice we cook with a couple of ingredients that appear frequently.

COCONUT OIL

A unique combination of fatty acids can have positive effects on health. This includes fat loss and better brain function. If you haven't cooked with coconut oil before, it's a treat. It's a great replacement for traditional oils and margarine. The oil stands up beautifully to high heat and the organic refined oil doesn't impart a strong coconut flavour or aroma. Of course, dependent on your choices, you can use other oils rapeseed, olive or real butter. Coconut oil works well in the recipes we have tried as it is often used as a bind with cacao.

FLAHAVAN'S IRISH PORRIDGE OATS

Flahavan's Irish Porridge Oats are the ideal ingredient for those wishing to incorporate oats into their diet. Flahavan's unique milling process retains the full rich texture of its plump Irish oats – sealing in the natural aroma - and giving its oats a distinctive creamy taste. Created using 100% natural Irish porridge oats, and with seven generations of milling experience Flahavan's Irish Porridge Oats are perfect for any mealtime – try our apple crumble for breakfast!

LINWOODS

Based in Armagh and established in 1965, Linwoods, like Slim's Healthy Kitchen, is a family owned company. Linwoods produce a range of healthy super food combinations that are stocked around the world. Milled Organic Flaxseed is one of nature's richest plant sources of omega 3. The flaxseeds are milled so that the nutritional benefits of the seeds can be easily absorb by the body, including iron, zinc, calcium, dietary fibre and omega 3. The milled chia seeds have an amazing nutritional offering, with omega 3, fibre, calcium, magnesium and phosphorus. The product is easily incorporated into a recipe or sprinkled over porridge, soups, and salads or thrown into shakes for added oomph.

The last two years for me have been an absolute whirlwind. We all have those bad days where we crave junk food but if this cookbook has done anything for me it has made me realise what I miss: really good, tasty healthy food. It has inspired me to get back in the kitchen to cook and if this book manages to help you eat healthy too then it's a success.

#IAMSLIM

BREAKFAST

AVOCADO BACON AND EGGS

❦ Avocados, yeah, they're fat, but they're the good kind of fat! ❦

SERVES 1

1 medium avocado

2 rashers cooked bacon, diced

2 medium eggs

paprika (optional)

Preheat the oven to 220°c and prepare a baking tray by lining with baking paper.

Slice the avocado down the centre and remove the pit. Gently spoon out a small amount of the avocado making the size of the hole left from the pit bigger.

Crack 1 egg into each half and top with bacon pieces. Sprinkle with paprika if desired. Bake for 15 minutes and grill under a medium heat for 2 minutes. Serve immediately.

BLUEBERRY MORNING MUFFINS

My son ate the whole plate of muffins when we made them.
That's how delicious they are.

12 SMALL MUFFINS

2 cups Flahavan's Irish
Porridge Oats

2 large bananas

2 medium eggs

½ cup low fat Greek yogurt

2 tbsp. agave

1 tbsp. baking powder

1 tbsp. baking soda

1 cup blueberries

1 tbsp. vanilla extract

Preheat oven to 180°c and set out 12 cupcake cases onto a baking tray or case tray.

In a food processor mix together Flahavan's Irish Porridge Oats, banana, eggs, yogurt, agave, baking powder, baking soda and vanilla extract until a smooth batter is formed.

Place the blueberries in a medium bowl, add the batter mix and gently combine.

Divide the mixture equally between the 12 cupcake cases. Bake for 20 minutes in a preheated oven.

Once golden on top remove from the oven and leave muffins to cool for 10 minutes before serving.

These muffins can be stored in an air tight container for up to 4 days.

BREAKFAST FRITTATA

❦ Make this into a lunch by throwing in some prawns and chorizo! ❦

SERVES 2

½ red onion, diced

1 red pepper, diced

1 yellow pepper, diced

½ tbsp. coconut oil

4 eggs, lightly beaten

1 chilli, chopped

4 rashers of bacon, grilled and diced

grated mozzarella, for decoration

Preheat grill to medium. In a medium frying pan (20cm) add coconut oil and heat the onion, peppers and bacon for 3 to 4 minutes, adding in chilli towards the end.

Take the pan off heat and drain out any excess oil that has formed.

Stir in the eggs and cook on a low heat for 15 minutes.

Finally finish under a heated grill to set the top, gently remove from the pan with a spatula or fish slice and serve immediately.

Sprinkle with grated mozzarella just before serving.

OVERNIGHT SLOW COOKED OATS

Save time in the morning before the school run by making this up before bed time and allowing it to cook over night, serve and go!

**SERVES 2-4
SMALL PORTIONS**

8 cups water

2 cups Flahavan's Irish Porridge Oats

½ cup dried cranberries

½ cup dried apricots, halved

pinch of salt

1 tbsp. ground cinnamon

1 tbsp. Linwoods Milled Chia Seed

In a slow cooker, add water, Flahavan's Irish Porridge Oats, cranberries, apricot, salt, Linwoods Milled Chia Seed and cinnamon.

Turn on to a low heat and place lid on.

Cook for 7 to 8 hours.

Serve topped with fresh fruit or a sprinkling of cinnamon.

Other ingredients could include apple pieces, raspberries, sliced banana, agave, vanilla extract, coconut, strawberries.

BACK TO PORRIDGE

Keep it simple by mixing two flavours as a serving suggestion.

SERVES 1

1 cup Flahavan's Irish
Porridge Oats

1½ cups of milk

pinch of salt

Add the Flahavan's Irish Porridge Oats, milk and salt to a large saucepan and stir gently over a medium heat.

Continuously stir for 5 to 6 minutes or until smooth and creamy. If you prefer your porridge not as thick, simply add small amounts of water and stir.

Here are a few suggestions of how you can add flavour to your porridge.

Apples and raspberries – after making your porridge, stir in ½ cup of grated apple over low heat and 2 tbsp of honey. Serve immediately placing raspberries on top and drizzle with more honey if desired.

Banana and cinnamon – after making your porridge, stir in 1 large banana chopped into thin slices and 1 tbsp of ground cinnamon powder. Keep on medium heat for 1 to 2 minutes then serve immediately.

QUINOA CAKES WITH SMOKED SALMON AND POACHED EGGS

A twist on eggs Benedict. Give it a try.

MAKES 6

2 cups cooked quinoa

1 tbsp. Linwoods Milled Organic Flaxseed

1 garlic clove, minced

1 tbsp. lemon zest

2 eggs, lightly beaten

1 tbsp. coconut oil

pinch salt and pepper

1 avocado, peeled and sliced

150g sliced smoked salmon

6 poached eggs

freshly chopped parsley

2 tbsp. water

In a large bowl, gently mix together quinoa, Linwoods Milled Organic Flaxseed, garlic, lemon zest and the lightly beaten eggs, adding in some salt and pepper for seasoning.

Add in 2 tbsp. of water to give the mixture a sticky consistency.

Divide the quinoa into 6 equally sized portions, roll into balls and set aside for cooking.

Prepare a medium pan over medium heat by coating it in coconut oil.

Add quinoa balls to the heated pan and gently flatten with a spatula, allow to cook on each side for 4-5 minutes or until golden brown.

As the quinoa cakes are cooking, prepare the poached eggs.

Fill a large pan with 5cm of water and heat until simmering and small bubbles appear through the water. Crack the eggs onto a plate one at a time and gently tip into the sauce pan.

Cooking for 3 minutes will leave a runny yolk perfect for this recipe.

Remove eggs from the water gently using a slotted spoon.

Divide the cooked quinoa cakes between plates, top with sliced avocado, sliced salmon and a poached egg . Serve garnished with fresh parsley.

RASPBERRY BREAKFAST BARS

Perfect for those mornings when you are on the go.

MAKES 10

2 ½ cups Flahavan's Irish Porridge Oats

1 cup smooth peanut butter

½ cup agave

¼ cup apple sauce

1 tbsp. ground cinnamon

1 large egg

⅓ cup sliced almonds

2 cups raspberries, quartered

2 tbsp. arrowstarch

1 tbsp. hot water

Preheat oven to 180°c and line a 10 x 10 inch (or similar) baking tray with baking paper.

To make the raspberry filling, in a small saucepan on a medium heat, mix together the raspberries and ¼ cup agave. Heat for 3 to 4 minutes or until boiling. Remove from heat and whisk in the arrowstarch and hot water until clump free. Set aside and leave to cool and thicken.

For the oat crumble, in a large bowl, mix together Flahavan's Irish Porridge Oats, peanut butter, agave, apple sauce, egg and ground cinnamon. Place ⅔ of the oat mixture evenly in the prepared baking tray. Making sure it is firmly pressed. On top of this evenly spread raspberry mix.

In a small bowl mix together the remaining oat mixture with the sliced almonds. Crumble this mixture on top of the raspberry layer pressing down to ensure it is well packed.

Bake for 30 minutes, the top will be golden brown. Leave to cool before cutting into desired square sizes. Can be stored in an air tight container for up to 5 days.

SMOOTHIES AND JUICES

EACH SMOOTHIE MAKES ONE JUICE

Take all your ingredients, throw them in a blender add some ice and mix it up until smooth.
Serve immediately

AVOCADO BOOST

1 avocado, pitted and skin removed

1 tbsp. agave

1 cup coconut milk

2 tbsp. freshly squeezed lime juice

PEACHY KEEN

1 large peach, peeled and seeded

½ cup raspberries

¾ cup low fat Greek yogurt

¼ cup almond milk

¼ cup orange juice

CHOCOLATE BANANA CAKE SHAKE

1 large banana

2 tbsp. cocoa powder

1½ cups milk
(soya, semi skimmed, full fat)

2 tbsp. smooth peanut butter

1 tbsp. Linwoods Milled Chia Seed

FOR THE FOLLOWING DRINKS, INSTEAD OF PUTTING ICE IN THE BLENDER SERVE POURED OVER ICE.

MORNING CHARGE

1 inch ginger, peeled

juice of half a lemon

2 cups carrots, peeled and chopped

½ cup fennel

LOWER THE BEET

2 apples, peeled and cored

½ cup pineapple

¼ cup beetroot

CUCUMBATADA

½ cucumber, peeled and sliced

1 inch ginger, peeled

1 pear, peeled and cored

½ cup kale

juice of half a lemon

WALNUT, RASPBERRY & ORANGE COUSCOUS

🌿 Come on, who doesn't like dessert for breakfast. 🌿

SERVES 2

½ cup walnuts

1½ cups couscous

½ tbsp ground cinnamon

4 mandarin oranges
(2 juiced and grated
zest and 2 sliced)

2 tbsp. honey

1 tbsp. coconut oil

1 cup raspberries

1 cup boiling water

fat free Greek yogurt for
serving (optional)

Preheat oven to 180°c, place walnuts on a baking tray and toast in preheated oven for 10 minutes, Once removed from the oven allow to cool then roughly chop.

Place grated orange zest and juice from 2 mandarins into a small pan over high heat. Add coconut oil and honey and boiling water. Once the contents are bubbling, remove from heat.

In a large mixing bowl, add couscous and cinnamon and pour over the boiling mixture. Cover with a tea towel and set aside.

Gently peel and slice the 2 remaining mandarins and sprinkle with a pinch of cinnamon.

Combine the sliced mandarins, raspberries and walnuts.

Fluff up the couscous with a fork and mix in the mandarins, raspberries and walnuts.

To serve drizzle with honey and a sprinkle of cinnamon and top with a dollop of Greek yogurt.

WHOLE WHEAT CHOCOLATE CHIP PANCAKES

❦ The perfect Sunday brunch. ❧

MAKES 6 TO 7 PANCAKES

½ cup chocolate chips

1 cup whole wheat flour

½ cup Flahavan's Irish Porridge Oats

pinch of salt

1 tbsp ground cinnamon

1½ tbsp baking powder

1 large egg

1 cup almond milk

1 tbsp brown sugar

¼ cup Greek yogurt

1 tbsp vanilla extract

agave and berries for serving

Mix together Flahavan's Irish Porridge Oats, flour, salt, cinnamon and baking powder in a large bowl and set aside.

In a smaller bowl mix together milk and egg, then add in the yogurt, brown sugar and vanilla and mix until well combined.

Making a well in the centre of the first bowl, slowly pour the liquid from the second bowl into this well. Stir gently until thoroughly mixed making sure not to over stir.

Add in the chocolate chips, or preferred fruit (blackberries, raspberries etc).

Heat a large pan or griddle and coat generously in coconut oil. Once hot, pour your desired amount of batter onto the pan to form your pancake. Cook until the edges form then flip over. Roughly 1 minute per side, turned 3 or 4 times.

Recoat pan with coconut oil for each individual pancake to avoid sticking.

Serve immediately topped with agave and berries.

LITE BITES

LiME BARBECUED PRAWNS

🌶 Throw another shrimp on the barbie! 🌶

SERVES 2-6

36 king prawns, peeled
and deveined

3 limes, grated and juiced

3 green chillies,
finely chopped

3 garlic cloves, mashed

1 inch piece
of ginger, grated

1 onion, finely diced

skewers

lettuce cup

In a food processor mix together ginger, garlic, onion, lime juice and chillies until smooth.

In a small bowl combine the prawns with grated lime and add in the smooth sauce. Cover with cling film or baking foil and refrigerate for 2 hours.

Remove from the fridge, and slide number of desired prawns onto each skewer and barbecue on a medium heat for 5 minutes. Turning throughout.

Remove from the barbecue and serve immediately on lettuce cups.

CARAMELISED RED ONION & MOZZARELLA TART

❧ Try hard not to eat this all yourself. ❧

SERVES 2

1 small red onion, diced

2 sheets filo pastry

6 cherry tomatoes, quartered

1½ cups mozzarella, roughly chopped

balsamic vinegar

coconut oil

pinch of salt and pepper

fresh parsley, to decorate

Preheat oven to 180°c and brush 2 tart dishes with coconut oil.

Fold each sheet of pastry so it is just larger than the tart dish, then push down into the tart dish. Cook in the oven until golden brown then set aside to cool.

In a pan soften the red onion in coconut oil and balsamic vinegar.

Place a handful of red onion in the dish then top with cherry tomatoes and mozzarella. Sprinkle more red onion on top and season with salt and pepper.

Place in oven and bake for 10 minutes.

Serve immediately with fresh parsley.

CAULIFLOWER GARLIC BREAD STICKS

If he doesn't kiss you when you've been
eating garlic, he doesn't love you!

MAKES 10-12

3 cups cauliflower rice
(1 small cauliflower, stalk
removed and blended in
a food processor)

3 cloves garlic, minced

1 egg, lightly beaten

1 cup grated mozzarella
plus 2 tbsp. for topping

1 tbsp. olive oil

pinch salt and pepper

1 tbsp. oregano

Preheat oven to 180°c and line a small loaf tin with baking paper.

In a small pan over low heat, mix together garlic and olive oil until hot, remove from heat and set aside.

In the oven heat the cauliflower rice for 6 minutes in an oven proof bowl covered with tin foil, then remove all moisture from the rice by squeezing it into a dry tea towel. The rice must be dry for the breadsticks to work.

In a large bowl, combine the rice, garlic, egg, mozzarella, oregano and salt and pepper.

Evenly spread the cauliflower mixture into the prepared loaf tin and bake until golden, 25 to 30 minutes.

Top with mozzarella and place under a medium grill for 5 minutes.

Remove the tin from the grill using oven gloves and gently lift the baking paper out of the loaf tin, slice into 1 inch wide slices and serve immediately.

CRUNCHY GARLIC MUSHROOMS WITH GARLIC AVOCADO AIOLI

🌿 See previous page! 🌿

10-12 medium mushrooms

¼ cup ground almonds

¼ cup ground hazelnuts

1 tbsp. arrowroot starch

1 tbsp. garlic powder

Pinch of salt and pepper

1 egg, lightly whisked

1 tbsp. coconut oil, melted

FOR THE GARLIC AVOCADO AIOLI

1 large avocado

⅓ cup low fat Greek yogurt

3 gloves garlic, mashed

pinch of salt and pepper

Preheat oven to 180°c and prepare a medium baking tray by lining with baking paper.

In a bowl mix together almonds, hazelnuts, garlic powder, salt and pepper.

Coat the mushrooms in arrowroot starch then dip in egg, and coat in the nut mixture.

Place mushrooms on baking tray and place in the oven for 15 minutes and prepare the garlic avocado aioli.

Place all the ingredients for the aioli in a food processor and blend until smooth.

Serve immediately.

LOADED NACHOS

Date night. Cinema night. Netflix and chill...

SERVES 4

2 large sweet potatoes

pinch of salt

2 chicken breasts, cooked and shredded

1 tbsp. olive oil

½ tbsp. garlic powder

½ tbsp. chilli powder

1 jalapeño, sliced

¼ red onion, sliced

1 cup guacamole (see sauces section)

1 cup salsa (see sauces section)

Preheat oven to 180°c and line a baking tray with baking paper

Slice sweet potatoes to roughly 0.5cm thick, spread evenly on to the baking tray and cook for 12 minutes or until crispy.

Remove from the oven and allow to cool.

In a bowl mix together chicken, olive oil, garlic, chilli, jalapeno and red onion until thoroughly combined.

Place the sweet potato chips on to a plate, top with salsa then the chicken mix and serve with a side of guacamole.

STUFFED ROMANO PEPPERS

These go really well with a flat grilled steak.

MAKES 8

4 Romano peppers, cut in half length ways

1 cup couscous

1 tbsp. coconut oil

400g turkey mince

1 medium onion, diced

1 tbsp. garlic powder

1 tbsp. cumin

1 tbsp. paprika

1 tbsp. cinnamon

1 tbsp. tomato paste

1 red chilli, finely chopped

1 tbsp. oregano

1 tbsp. fresh parsley, finely chopped

Preheat oven to 180°c and prepare a baking tray by lining with baking paper.

Place peppers on prepared tray and cook in the oven for 10 minutes. During this time prepare the couscous.

In a bowl add boiling water to the couscous covering it by an inch. Cover with a tea towel and leave for 10 minutes. Drain excess water and leave until ready for use.

In a large pan heat coconut oil over medium heat. Add cumin, paprika, garlic, cinnamon and onions to the pan and stir until onions are soft.

Add turkey mince, tomato paste and chilli. Keep stirring gently breaking up the turkey until the meat is cooked through. Stir in the cooked couscous, parsley and oregano and combine.

Spoon the turkey mixture into the peppers and return to the oven for 15 minutes.

Top with fresh parsley and serve immediately.

SUPER LEMON HUMMUS

🌶 It's tangy with a kick! 🌶

1 cup canned
chickpeas, drained

3 tbsp freshly squeezed
lemon juice

1 tbsp lemon zest

2 garlic cloves, mashed

1 tbsp ground cumin

pinch salt

3 tbsp water

1 tbsp chilli powder

3 tbsp extra virgin olive oil

Place all the ingredients in a food processor and mix until smooth.

Refrigerate for an hour to set then serve.

Serving suggestions include flat bread, warmed pitta bread, sweet potato chips or coat a chicken breast with the hummus and bake in the oven.

Store in an air tight container in the fridge for up to 3 days.

SWEET POTATO BITES

Just like mini sweet potato pizzas.

15-20 BITES

2 large sweet potatoes, sliced into 1cm thick slices

1 avocado, pitted

1 tbsp. paprika

salt

¼ cup fresh squeezed lime juice (2 limes)

6 cherry tomatoes, sliced

1 red onion, finely sliced

watercress for decoration

olive oil

Preheat oven to 200°c and prepare a baking tray by lining with baking paper.

In a large bowl mix together the sweet potato slices, paprika, pinch of salt and olive oil.

Place the sweet potato slices on the prepared baking tray and place in oven for 15 minutes. Whilst the sweet potato is cooking prepare the avocado topping.

Scoop the avocado into a medium bowl and mix in the lime juice and ½ teaspoon of salt and mash together.

Top each sweet potato slice with a spoonful of avocado, top with a tomato slice and red onion. Add a few stalks of watercress for decoration.

Serve immediately.

SOUPS,
SALADS
& SAUCES

SUPER GREEN QUINOA SALAD

🌱 It's pronounced... keen-wa! 🌱

SERVES 2

2 cups kale, thinly torn

1 cup basil leaves, chopped

⅓ cup pistachios, chopped

1 avocado, pitted and the inside cubed

2 tbsp. olive oil

juice of ½ a lemon

1½ cups cooked quinoa

½ red onion finely sliced

pinch of salt and pepper

In a large bowl mix together kale, basil, olive oil, lemon juice and seasoning, making sure all ingredients are thoroughly combined.

Add in quinoa, red onion and avocado and continue to gently combine all the ingredients.

Immediately serve and sprinkle with pistachios.

HONEY BAKED CHICKEN WITH CUCUMBER AND PEACH SALAD

🌿 Turn this into a main course by adding clean carbs. 🌿

SERVES 4

4 chicken breasts

2 tbsp. coconut oil

5 tbsp. agave

1 tbsp. sesame seeds

2 baby gem lettuces leaves removed.

2 tbsp. olive oil

2 peaches, peeled and sliced

1 lime, grated zest and squeezed for juice

1 cucumber, peeled and sliced

Preheat oven to 200°c and prepare a baking tray with baking paper.

In a medium frying pan add coconut oil and when hot add chicken and cook until lightly browned.

After 5 minutes and chicken is lightly brown all over, transfer to the prepared baking tray and pour 4 tablespoons of agave generously over chicken and coat with sesame seeds. Place in oven for 15 minutes and make the salad.

To make the salad, mix together the sliced cucumber, peaches, and lime zest.

In a separate bowl combine 1 tablespoon agave, lime juice and olive oil and toss with the lettuce.

Divide the lettuce, between serving plates and top with the cucumber mix and add the honey baked chicken.

Why not try sprinkling with some pomegranate seeds for added flavour.

GRiLLED SALMON NiÇOiSE SALAD

❥ The trick to perfecting this recipe is to keep your eggs runny and soft. ❦

SERVES 4

FOR THE DRESSING

2 tbsp. Dijon mustard

½ cup extra virgin olive oil

3 tbsp. white wine

2 tbsp. agave

pinch of salt and pepper

FOR THE SALAD

2 salmon fillets

1 tbsp. coconut oil

1 tbsp. olive oil

300g boiled baby
potatoes, some halved
some quartered

200g green beans

4 medium eggs

½ cup red onion, thinly sliced

1 cup cherry tomatoes,
quartered

1 cup romaine lettuce leaves

½ cup olives, pitted
and halved

FOR THE DRESSING

Mix together Dijon mustard, white wine and agave and add your preferred amount of salt and pepper to season.

Gradually add in the olive oil whilst slowly whisking the dressing.

Set aside and prepare the salad

FOR THE SALAD

Place eggs in a saucepan and boil to your preferred texture. Remove shell, leave to cool, cut into quarters and set aside.

Preheat grill to medium and brush the grill shelf with coconut oil for the salmon.

Mix green beans and potatoes in olive oil and season with salt and pepper and set aside.

Place potatoes in the grill, cut side down to start and turn after 10 mins. Repeat until lightly charred and soft on the inside. Add the green beans and leave for 3-4 minutes. Turning once.

Finally add your salmon and grill for 3-4 minutes each side or until thoroughly cooked.

Whilst salmon is grilling, divide the lettuce, tomatoes, onion, eggs and olives between four plates. Add green beans, potatoes and salmon and drizzle with the dressing.

GINGER STEAK SALAD

🌶 A man's salad. 🌶

SERVES 2

For the marinade

1 10oz sirloin steak

¼ cup soy sauce

1 inch piece of ginger, grated

2 red chillies, chopped

2 garlic cloves, minced

1 lime, juiced

For the dressing

1 tbsp. coconut oil, melted

2 tbsp. fish sauce

2 tbsp. soy sauce

pinch brown sugar

1 lime, zest and juiced

1 chilli, chopped

Salad

2 baby gem lettuces, chopped

1 red bell pepper, roughly chopped

1 cucumber, sliced

handful of peanuts

In a medium bowl combine all of the marinade ingredients omitting the steak. Once thoroughly combined, place steak in the bowl, covering with the marinade. Cover the bowl with cling film and place in the fridge overnight.

For the dressing, mix together the ingredients in a small bowl and set in the fridge for 15 minutes to chill.

Cook the steak how you prefer, we would suggest medium which is approximately 11 minutes turning occasionally. Leave the steak to rest for 10 minutes after cooking then slice.

In a large bowl, mix together lettuce, pepper, and cucumber. Add in the dressing and toss together again.

To serve arrange the salad on to a plate, top with sliced steak and sprinkle with peanuts, if desired.

COOLING CUCUMBER SOUP

A refreshing cool-down soup.

SERVES 2

2 cups of peeled
and sliced cucumber

1 cup water

2 cups low fat Greek yogurt

1 onion, diced

1 tbsp dijon mustard

3 tbsp fresh dill

1 tbsp fresh parsley

Add all the ingredients to a food processor
and blend until smooth but still thick.

Transfer to a large bowl and refrigerate for 5 hours.
This is necessary to set the consistency of the
soup and bring out the flavour.

Serve immediately sprinkled with fresh dill,
and thin cucumber slices.

CREAMY CAULIFLOWER SOUP

Creamy without the cream.

SERVES 2

2 cups cauliflower, diced

1 onion, diced

2 garlic cloves, minced

½ tbsp. olive oil

2 tbsp. grated parmesan (optional)

3 cups vegetable broth, see recipe below

pinch of salt

In a large soup pot, heat olive oil and soften the onion and garlic.

Add vegetable broth and cauliflower and simmer for 20 minutes.

Add the soup with a pinch of salt to a food processor and blend until smooth.

Serve immediately and top with grated Parmesan if desired.

VEGETABLE BROTH

1 onion, diced

3 stalks of celery, sliced

2 carrots, peeled and sliced

⅓ cup mushrooms, halved

3 cloves garlic, halved

7 cups of water

Place all the ingredients in a large soup pot over medium heat and bring to the boil.

Reduce to a lower heat and simmer for 1 hour.

Serve immediately as a soup on its own or use in the recipe above.

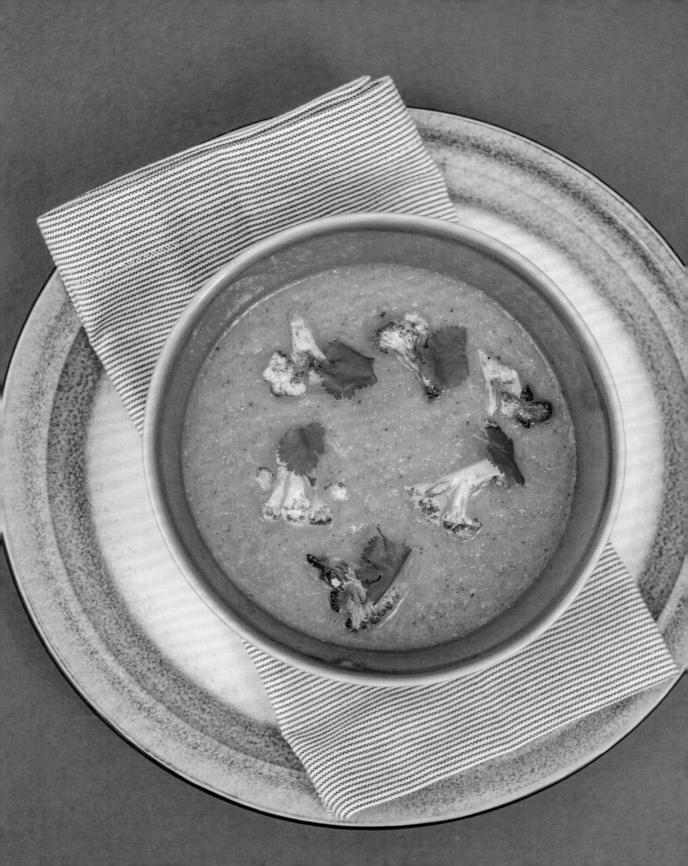

GINGER AND CARROT SOUP WITH A GARLIC CASHEW CREAM

Up the cashews to get them protein gains.

FOR THE SOUP

1 cup onion, diced

2 tbsp. ginger, grated

½ tbsp. ground cinnamon

2 tbsp. coconut oil

2 cloves garlic, minced

1 tbsp. ground turmeric

½ tbsp. salt

pinch ground
cayenne pepper

2 cups carrots, sliced

4 cups water

FOR THE CASHEW CREAM

1½ cup cashews
(soaked overnight in water)

1 cup water

2 gloves garlic, minced

1 tbsp. cayenne pepper

In a food processor blend the soaked cashews until smooth, add in water, garlic and cayenne pepper. Blend until all ingredients are thoroughly combined. Set aside for later.

Soften onion in coconut oil in a large soup pan for 5-6 minutes. Add garlic, ginger, turmeric, cinnamon, cayenne and salt stirring, as each ingredient is added.

Add in carrots and water and bring to the boil then reduce heat and let simmer for 15 minutes or until the carrots are soft.

Pour soup into a food processor and add ¼ of the cashew cream. Blend then return to soup pan and further heat for 10 minutes.

Serve immediately by dividing between bowls and drizzling with the remaining cashew cream.

BROCCOLI SOUP WiTH STiLTON CRUMB

We were generous with the stilton
but it was all for the photo...promise!

2 cups broccoli,
stalks removed

2 tbsp. coconut oil

½ cup sliced celery

½ cup sliced leek

½ cup peeled
boiled potatoes

1 litre of vegetable broth
(see page 66)

1 tbsp. butter

1 onion, finely diced

1 cup stilton, crumbled

fresh parsley for decoration

In a large pan add the onion to coconut oil over medium heat and cook until soft. Add in celery, leek, potato and butter, stir until combined and melted. Leave to heat for 5 minutes.

Add the vegetable broth and any larger bits of broccoli and cook on a low heat for 12 minutes before adding the smaller bits of broccoli and cook for a further 5 minutes.

Transfer carefully to a food processor and blend until smooth.

Serve immediately, topping with a handful of crumbled stilton and fresh parsley. The stilton is optional but does add a great creamy taste to the soup.

SOME SiMPLE SAUCES

GUACAMOLE

2 avocados, pitted
3 tomatoes, chopped
2 cloves garlic, mashed
pinch of salt
juice of 1 lime

-

Scoop avocado into a mixing bowl, add in tomatoes, garlic, salt and lime juice and mash together with a fork. Set in the fridge for an hour before use and keep any leftover refrigerated in an airtight container for up to 3 days.

CHIMICHURRI

2 tbsp. parsley, finely chopped
1 clove garlic, minced
2 tbsp. apple cider vinegar
2 tbsp. coriander, finely chopped
2 tbsp. extra virgin olive oil
2 tbsp. red onion, finely diced
pinch salt and pepper
1 tbsp. water
½ tbsp. red pepper flakes
Pinch chilli flakes

-

In a small bowl mix together red onion, olive oil, vinegar and salt and allow to sit for 15 minutes.

Add in the remaining ingredients and stir gently.

Can be used immediately or stored in the fridge in an airtight container for up to 5 days.

SALSA

3 cups chopped tomatoes
1 cup onion, diced
½ green bell pepper, diced
¼ cup fresh coriander, chopped
2 tbsp. fresh lime juice
1 jalapeno, finely chopped
1 tbsp ground cumin
pinch salt and black pepper

-

In a large bowl gently combine all ingredients, refrigerate and allow to marinate overnight. Can be kept in an airtight container in the fridge for up to 5 days.

GARLIC PESTO

3 garlic cloves, mashed
1 cup fresh coriander
1 tbsp. salt
¼ cup fresh lime juice
½ cup cashew nuts, soaked in water for 2 hours and drained before use

-

Place all the ingredients in a food processor and blend until smooth.

Place in the fridge to set for an hour before use. Can be stored in an airtight container in the fridge for up to 3 days.

MAINS

FALAFEL BURGERS WITH SWEET POTATO FRIES

🌱 You'll never know this ain't meat. 🌿

SERVES 4

FOR THE BURGERS

2 cups chickpeas, drained and dried

1 onion, finely chopped

2 garlic cloves, mashed

2 tbsp. almond flour

2 tbsp. ground cumin

1 tbsp. ground coriander

1 tbsp. fresh chopped parsley

2 tbsp. coconut oil

4 Romaine lettuce leaves

½ cup super lemon hummus (see page 51)

watercress

FOR THE SWEET POTATO FRIES

5 large sweet potatoes

2 tbsp. rapeseed oil

pinch of salt and pepper

pinch of garlic powder

pinch of paprika

FALAFEL BURGERS

Blend chickpeas in a food processor until a crumb like mixture forms.

Add in onion, garlic, almond flour, cumin, coriander and parsley and blend until well combined.

Remove from the food processor and using your hands form 4 patties from the mixture around 2cm in thickness.

In a large pan, heat coconut oil and cook the falafel burgers for 2 minutes each side.

To serve lay the falafel burger on the lettuce leaf, top with a layer of evenly spread hummus adding a handful of watercress.

TO MAKE THE SWEET POTATO FRIES

Preheat oven to 200°c and line a baking tray with baking paper.

Mix rapeseed oil, garlic, salt, pepper and paprika in a bowl and set aside.

Wash and peel the sweet potatoes before cutting into ¼ inch fries.

Brush the sweet potato fries in the rapeseed oil mix and place on baking tray.

Cook for 25 minutes, turning half way through

Once cooked, remove from the oven and serve immediately.

HONEY BAKED GARLIC CHICKEN

A takeaway favourite that you can now
make at home, healthier and tastier.

SERVES 2-4

450g boneless chicken
breasts, diced into small
1 inch pieces.

4 cloves garlic, minced

2 large eggs, beaten

⅓ cup agave

2 tbsp. soy sauce

1 tbsp. corn starch

pinch of salt and black
pepper

2 tbsp sesame seeds

1 cup panko breadcrumbs

rice to serve

coconut oil

water

Preheat oven to 220°c and lightly brush an oven
dish with coconut oil.

Season the chicken with salt and pepper then dip into the
beaten egg to coat then cover in panko bread crumbs.

Add chicken pieces to the prepared baking dish and place
in the oven for 15-20 minutes until golden and crisp.

In a medium saucepan over high heat, mix the honey,
garlic and soy sauce.

In a small bowl combine the corn starch and ⅓ cup of water.

Stir the corn starch mixture into the saucepan gradually until
thickened, roughly 2-3 minutes. Add chicken and gently mix.

Serve immediately on a bed of rice and garnish
with sesame seeds.

ITALIAN BITES WITH COURGETTE NOODLES

SERVES 2-4

For the Bites

1½ cans of cannellini beans

1 roasted red bell pepper, roughly chopped

½ onion, grated

2 gloves garlic, minced

¼ cup parsley, chopped

1 tbsp. oregano

½ cup dried breadcrumbs

pinch salt and pepper

fresh basil, for serving

coconut oil

1 medium egg

For the Sauce

⅔ cups chopped tomatoes

1 glove garlic, minced

tbsp of finely sliced ginger

1 tbsp tomato paste

pinch oregano

pinch basil

2 tbsp. balsamic vinegar

For the Noodles

1 large courgette

For the Bites

Preheat oven to 180°c and coat a large baking tray with coconut oil.

Mix together cannellini beans and roasted red pepper in a food processor. Mix to a chunky consistency, not a smooth puree.

Transfer mixture to a medium bowl and then add in grated onion, garlic, parsley, oregano, egg, breadcrumbs, salt and pepper and mix thoroughly.

Using your hands, roll the mixture in your palms until you achieve a ball like shape and place on the prepared baking tray.

Bake the bites for 20 minutes until firm and golden. During this time prepare the sauce and courgette noodles.

For the Sauce

Place all the listed ingredients into a food processor and mix on a slow speed until a thick sauce is formed.

Remove the sauce from the food processor and transfer to a saucepan and gently heat over a medium heat, not allowing it to boil.

For the Courgette Noodles

Us a spiralizer or a julienne peeler, to create noodles from the courgette.

Place noodles in a medium saucepan on a high heat for 5 to 6 minutes, or until soft.

To serve divide noodles between serving plates, adding the Itallian bites and sauce and top with a piece of fresh basil.

SLOW COOKED THAI BEEF

This will take all the stress out of cooking. Prepare and turn on at lunch time and it will be ready to serve for a dinner party or post gym meal.

SERVES 4

2 tbsp. coconut oil

1kg diced beef brisket

¼ cup coriander, roughly chopped

2 garlic cloves, mashed

1 green chilli, chopped

2 stalks of lemongrass, 1 mashed and 1 chopped

1cm piece of ginger, peeled and chopped

50ml apple cider vinegar

50ml fish sauce

1 tbsp. light brown sugar

200g can of coconut milk, stirred before use

1 whole star anise

1 tbsp. paprika

juice of 1 lime

In a large frying pan heat 1 tbsp. coconut oil and brown off the beef, keeping any juices from the pan for use later and set aside beef to cool.

Place coriander, chopped lemongrass, ginger, garlic and chilli and 1 tbsp. of coconut oil in a blender and mix until a paste forms.

Turn the slow cooker to low heat and add in the paste, beef and any juices kept from earlier along with the rest of the ingredients minus the lime juice.

Cook for 6-8 hours. This will depend on the size of the beef pieces. The meat will be ready when it is soft and almost falling apart.

Serve immediately with a side of rice and a squeeze of lime juice.

SWEET POTATO PiZZA

🌿 The perfect treat night pizza without making it a cheat night! 🌿

SERVES 2-4

For the Pizza

⅔ sweet potatoes, you will need enough to make 1 cup of sweet potato mash

1 cup almond flour

1 tbsp. baking soda

1 tbsp. oregano

1 tbsp. salt

For the Sauce

¼ cup olive oil

5 cloves garlic, minced

1 can chopped tomatoes, blended

1 tbsp. dried basil

½ tbsp. dried oregano

pinch dried thyme

pinch salt and pepper

top with your favourite pizza toppings, we've used cherry tomatoes, mixed peppers and chorizo. We prefer Mozzarella cheese to cheddar.

FOR THE PIZZA

Preheat oven to 200°c and prepare a large saucepan with boiling water.

Peel and cut each sweet potato into 4 and place in the saucepan over a high heat. Boil for 20 minutes or until soft when pierced with a knife.

Drain potatoes and mash well then place into a large bowl and leave to cool. Mix together one cup of sweet potato, almond flour, baking soda, oregano and salt. Knead well together until it forms a dough like ball.

Line a large tray with baking paper and press the dough out into a large circle. Roughly ½ inch thick.

Place in the oven and bake for 12 minutes, until the edges are slightly browned. Prepare your pizza sauce while your base is baking.

FOR THE PIZZA SAUCE

Heat olive oil in a small pan over high heat. Once hot add garlic and move to a medium heat so as the garlic doesn't burn.

Transfer the garlic oil to a medium bowl and stir in tomatoes and seasoning.

Evenly spread the sauce onto the pizza base, top with mozzarella and your desired toppings and return to the oven for 5 minutes.

SALMON QUINOA BURGERS

*Never eat anything you can't pronounce,
except quinoa. Eat quinoa.*

SERVES 4-6

16oz wild salmon fillet
skin removed

1 tbsp. coconut oil

⅓ cup onion, diced

1 cup kale, finely chopped

salt and pepper for seasoning

¾ cup cooked quinoa

2 tbsp. mustard

1 large egg

FOR THE SALAD

2 tbsp. lemon juice

2 tbsp. Dijon mustard

1 avocado, peeled
and roughly diced

100g cherry tomato

100g watercress

1 lemon

Cut off roughly a 4oz piece of salmon in a food processor to finely chop. This is used to hold the burgers together.

Using a knife, finely chop the remaining salmon and move to a large bowl.

Using medium heat, heat a skillet and oil, kale and onions. Add seasoning and cook until tender. Roughly 5 to 6 minutes.

Transfer to the large bowl with the salmon, adding in the cooked quinoa, mustard and egg.

Using your hands combine the ingredients together, then form into 5 patties.

Lightly heat a non-stick grill pan, add a splash of coconut oil and gently cook the salmon burgers for 4-5 minutes each side, turning regularly.

Meanwhile mix the lemon juice and mustard and some salt and pepper and set aside.

Mix the avocado, tomatoes and watercress and divide between plates. Add salmon burger, drizzle with dressing and add extra lemon wedges for squeezing

SPEEDY CHICKEN RAMEN

Our favourite quick winter recipe. Warming and extremely filling.

SERVES 2

2 chicken breasts, cooked and sliced

1 litre chicken stock

3 red chillies, chopped

300ml water

pinch of salt and pepper

¼ cup chopped coriander

2 tbsp. light soy sauce

1 cup mushrooms, halved

100g baby pak choi

100g egg noodles

1 cup sliced bamboo shoots

In a large saucepan over medium heat, add the chicken stock, half of the coriander and the chilli. Bring to the boil and add 300ml of water. Once bubbling reduce the heat and allow to simmer.

Add in the soy sauce, pinch of salt and pepper, mushrooms, pak choi and egg noodles, boil for 2 minutes before lowering heat and adding the bamboo shoots for 4 minutes.

Serve immediately into bowls and top with the remaining coriander.

PESTO SALMON

Stick in the oven and away you go!

SERVES 4

4 salmon fillets

2 cups cherry
tomatoes, halved

16 asparagus tips

juice of 1 lemon

½ cup pesto

pinch of salt and pepper

2 tbsp. olive oil

Preheat oven to 200°c and prepare tinfoil packages by cutting pieces into 15 inch squares, this is to wrap the salmon in for cooking.

In a bowl mix together asparagus, olive oil and salt and pepper. Divide the asparagus by placing 4 into each tinfoil package.

Place the salmon on top of the asparagus and top with pesto and a drizzle of lemon juice.

Loosely wrap the package and place in the oven and cook for 25 minutes until salmon is cooked through.

Remove immediately and serve with a side of baby potatoes.

ORANGE BAKED SEA BASS

*If you would like to make this paleo,
you just need a sharp stick and a stone.*

SERVES 2-4

3 whole sea bass,
approximately 300g each

4 tbsp. olive oil

pinch sea salt

pinch black pepper

3 tbsp. sesame
seeds, toasted

1 inch piece of
ginger, grated

½ tbsp. chilli flakes

¼ cup freshly squeezed
orange juice

⅓ cup orange, finely diced
to a pulp

zest from one orange

rice for serving

Preheat oven to 220°c and line a baking tray with tinfoil.

Place the fish onto the tin foil evenly spaced and coat with olive oil, sea salt, pepper and sesame seeds. Cover with tinfoil and bake in oven for 25 minutes.

As the fish is cooking, in a pan over medium heat combine the ginger, chilli flakes, freshly squeezed orange juice, orange pulp and orange zest.

Bring saucepan to the boil then reduce heat and simmer for 10 minutes.

Remove the fish from the oven and serve immediately on a bed of rice, drizzled with orange sauce.

CRUNCHY BEEF STIRFRY

🌶 We guarantee this will taste better than any takeaway! 🌶

SERVES 2-4

400g diced beef

1 cup baby corn

1 cup broccoli, chopped

½ cup green beans

juice of 1 lime and 1 lime, cut into wedges

300g ready cooked rice noodles

1 tbsp. coconut oil

3 tbsp. soy sauce

2 tbsp. fish sauce

1 inch piece of ginger, grated

In a bowl soften the noodles in boiling water, drain then set aside and cover with a tea towel to use later.

Add the coconut oil to a wok pan over high heat and mix in the diced beef, cook until brown then mix in the broccoli, baby corn and green beans.

Remove from heat and gently pour in the soy sauce, fish sauce and lime juice before returning to a medium heat for 4 minutes.

Divide the noodles between plates and top with the beef stir fry mix and serve with a wedge of lime.

COURGETTE LASAGNE

A healthier alternative to an old family favourite!

SERVES 4-6

2 courgettes, sliced

1 ball mozzarella, thinly sliced

½ cup cherry tomatoes, halved

500g steak mince

1 onion, diced

1 red pepper, finely diced

1 tbsp. coconut oil

1 cup beef stock

Preheat oven to 200˚c and brush a medium dish with coconut oil or 4 smaller individual dishes if preferred.

In a frying pan over medium heat, soften the onion in the coconut oil until brown. Add the diced pepper and cook for 4 minutes.

Add the mince to the pan and gently stir until browned. Pour in the beef stock, cover and simmer over a low heat for 30 minutes.

Once ready, spoon the mince mixture into the prepared dish to ¼ full. Top with a slice of courgette and then a slice of mozzarella. Add a few cherry tomatoes.

Top with another layer of mince, a slice of courgette and some cherry tomatoes and place in the oven for 15 minutes.

Finish under a medium heated grill for 5 minutes and serve immediately.

SWEET POTATO PiE

Perfect for making in advance and re-heating for a midweek meal.

SERVES 4-6

500g extra lean mince beef

800ml organic beef stock

2 onions, finely diced

3 carrots, finely diced

3 garlic cloves, grated

2 tbsp. rapeseed oil

4 sweet potatoes, peeled and quartered

2 tbsp. parmesan cheese

pinch of black pepper

In a large pan over medium heat soften the onion in the rapeseed oil until golden brown. Add in carrots and garlic and cook for 5 minutes.

Stir in the mince and cook until brown then gradually add in the organic beef stock gently stirring as you do so.

Cover and allow to simmer for 30 minutes.

As this simmers, place the sweet potatoes in a large pan of boiling water and boil for 20 minutes until soft.

Drain and mash the sweet potato, adding in black pepper and half of the Parmesan as you mash.

Spoon the mince into a large oven dish,and top with the mashed sweet potato and place under the grill on medium heat for 10 minutes. Remove and sprinkle with the remaining parmesan and return to the grill for a further 4 minutes.

Serve immediately with a side of vegetables.

WARMING FISH CURRY

This recipe will work with a variety of fish types.

SERVES 2-3

2 tbsp. coconut oil

600g cod fillets,
diced into 2cm cubes

1 onion, diced

1 inch piece of ginger grated

2 garlic cloves mashed

2 tbsp curry powder

2 cups chopped tomatoes

1 tbsp. tomato puree

¾ cup fish stock

pinch salt and pepper

¼ cup fat free Greek yogurt

rice to serve

Melt the coconut oil in a large frying pan over a medium heat and add the onion. Cook until lightly browned and soft then add in the garlic and ginger. Stir until the 3 ingredients are combined then add in the curry powder.

Add in the chopped tomatoes, fish stock and tomato puree and gently stir together. Allow to simmer over a low heat for 20 minutes.

Finally add in the cod and mix through. Cover with a lid and allow to cook on a low heat for 15 minutes. Making sure the fish is thoroughly cooked.

Serve immediately onto a bed of rice. Or refrigerate for up to 3 days or freeze in an air tight container for later use.

BEEFY LETTUCE CUPS

🌱 Easy as... 1,2,3. 🥄

SERVES 2-4

500g lean steak mince

1 tbsp. olive oil

1 onion, diced

3 gloves garlic,
finely chopped

1 inch piece of
ginger, grated

½ cup water
chestnuts, chopped

4 tbsp. hoisin sauce

1 tbsp. soy sauce

1 carrot, grated

2 tbsp. sesame seeds,
toasted

Romaine lettuce leaves,
for serving

In a frying over medium heat, add olive oil and stir in the steak mince. Fry until brown and cooked through then set aside on a plate for later.

In the same pan cook the onion, garlic and ginger until soft. Return the cooked steak mince to the pan adding in water chestnuts.

Stir the hoisin sauce and soy sauce into the mixture and allow to simmer for 4 minutes.

Serve immediately by placing the steak mince in a romaine lettuce leaf and topping with grated carrot and sesame seeds.

SWEET TREATS

CHOCOLATE CHIP BANANA BREAD

For a fruitier alternative why not replace the chocolate chips with some berries or omit them altogether. Tastes just as good!

½ cup of dark chocolate chips

2 medium sized bananas, mashed

½ cup coconut flour

½ cup almond meal

4 medium eggs

2 tbsp. unsweetened apple sauce

3 tbsp. melted coconut oil

2 tbsp. agave

2 tbsp. vanilla extract

pinch baking soda

Prepare a small loaf tin by lining with baking paper and set aside.

Preheat oven to 180°c.

In a large mixing bowl mix together the mashed bananas, agave, coconut oil, chocolate chips, apple sauce, eggs and vanilla extract until thoroughly combined.

To this mixture add the coconut flour, almond meal and baking soda. Leave to rest for 3 to 4 minutes. As the mixture rests it will thicken. If you feel your mixture is too runny gradually add in more coconut flour, a teaspoon at a time until the desired texture is achieved.

Pour your mixture into the prepared loaf tin and bake in the oven for 35 to 40 minutes. A good way to test your loaf is cooked right through is to pierce it with a skewer and if the skewer comes out mixture free and clean your bread is ready to serve. If you find your bread is browning too much on top during baking. Remove from oven and cover with cooking foil and return for the duration.

Bread can be served warm or cold but will slice easier if left to cool.

RASPBERRY CAKE

Keep this in the freezer just before serving.

1 cup almonds

1 cup dates

½ desiccated coconut

¾ cup coconut milk

2 cups cashews soaked overnight or in hot water for 2 hours

3 tbsp. coconut oil, melted

½ cup agave

juice of 1 lemon

1 tbsp. vanilla essence

2 cups raspberries

Line a medium loaf tin with cling film.

In a food processor mix together almonds, dates, and coconut until the mixture comes to a sticky dough.

Evenly press the mixture into the loaf tin to form the base.

Place the cashews, coconut milk, coconut oil, agave and juice of 1 lemon into the food processor and blend until smooth.

Stir in the vanilla essence and pour ⅔ of this mixture on top of the base. Press half of the raspberries into the 2nd layer and place in the freezer for 10 minutes

Add the remaining raspberries to the rest of the mixture and blend together.

Pour raspberry mixture over the 2nd layer and smooth out. Return to the freezer and set for 2 hours.

Slice to serve and store in the freezer.

CREAMY BLACKBERRY BARS

Look at the pic, just look at it...

MAKES 12

1 cup of pitted
Medjool dates

2 cups of walnuts

pinch of Himalayan salt

1½ cups of blackberries

2 cups cashew nuts
(cashews must be soaked
overnight in water to
help form the smooth
creamy texture)

⅓ cup agave

½ cup melted coconut oil

15 blackberries for
decoration

For the base add dates, walnuts and salt into a food processor and mix until a smooth but sticky dough like texture forms.

Use a 14 x 11 inch deep sided baking tray lined with baking paper, press out your mixture evenly to form the base.

Place baking tray into the freezer as you make the top layer.

For the top layer place cashew nuts, agave, coconut oil, blackberries and pinch of salt into a food processor and blend until smooth and creamy.

Remove baking tray from the freezer and pour mixture onto the base evening out with a spatula.

Place tray into the fridge and chill for 3 hours.

Gently remove from baking tray and cut into squares, decorate with blackberries and enjoy.

Store in fridge for 2 to 3 days.

MINT BITES

We aren't telling you what time is best to eat these, but try after 8!

MAKES 12

For the mint base

1 cup cashews, soaked overnight or in boiling water for 2 hours

1 cup spinach

¼ cup coconut oil, melted

½ cup coconut milk

¼ cup desiccated coconut

1 tbsp. peppermint essence

¼ cup mint leaves

For the chocolate topping

1 cup coconut oil, melted

½ cup cacao powder

2 tbsp. agave

In a food processor, blend together cashews, coconut oil, and coconut milk until smooth.

Add in the spinach, mint, coconut and peppermint essence and blend again until everything is smooth and runny.

Pour this mixture into silicone cupcake cases leaving room at the top for a layer of chocolate. Refrigerate for 15 minutes.

In a bowl mix together the chocolate topping ingredients, stirring until smooth.

Remove the cupcake cases from the freezer and top with a layer of the chocolate mix.

Return to the freezer and allow to set for 2 hours, once set the mint bites can be stored in the freezer for up to 5 days.

HONEY AND CiNNAMON ENERGY BiTES

❧ Keep them small and bite size. ❧

MAKES 12

2 cups Flahavan's Irish Porridge Oats

1 cup almond butter

3 tbsp. coconut oil

2 tbsp. ground cinnamon

3 tbsp. Linwoods Milled Organic Flaxseed

2 tbsp. Linwoods Milled Chai Seed

1 cup dark chocolate chips

1/4 cup of honey

Melt coconut oil gently over a low heat. Be careful it does not get too hot and turn brown.

Add all ingredients into a large bowl and using your hands gently combine all the ingredients.

Place mixture in the fridge to chill for an hour, this will make it easier to shape.

When chilled remove from fridge and mould into small balls around 2cm in diameter by rolling the mixture together in your hands.

Place on a tray and store in the fridge until required. These can be stored in an airtight container in the fridge for up to 5 days.

KEY LIME AVOCADO CHEESECAKE

It sounds so wrong, but this is
the first recipe you should make!

SERVES 6

¾ cup Flahavan's Irish
Porridge Oats

¾ cup walnuts plus a
handful for decoration

6 medjool dates pitted

2 tbsp. almond milk

3 avocados

¼ cup fresh squeezed
lime juice

3 tbsp. agave

1 tbsp. coconut oil

1 tbsp. lime zest

Line a 20 cm cake tin with baking paper.

Place Flahavan's Irish Porridge Oats, walnuts,
dates and almond milk into a food processor
and blend until a sticky mixture forms.

Press this mixture into the cake tin creating an even base
and place in the freezer before preparing the top layer.

Remove the pit and scoop out the inside of the avocado
and place in a food processor along with lime juice, agave,
coconut oil and lime zest and blend until smooth.

Pour the smooth avocado mix over the base layer
and smooth out with the back of a spoon.

Place cake tin back into the freezer to set for 2 hours.
Once set gently push the cake out of the cake tin
and remove baking paper. Decorate with a few walnuts
and serve. Store any leftovers in the freezer.

MATCHA GREEN TEA BITES

They'll turn you green just like The Hulk.

MAKES 6

1 cup Medjool dates, pitted

½ cup almonds

¼ cup cacao powder

2 tbsp. matcha green tea powder, plus extra for dusting

1 tbsp. almond milk

In a food processor mix together the dates and almonds until a sticky texture is formed.

Add cacao powder, matcha green tea and almond milk and mix again.

Remove the mixture from the food processor and break off a small amount and roll into a ball using your hands. Repeat until all the mixture is used.

Finish off the balls with a dusting of matcha green tea powder. Store in an airtight container in the fridge for up to 5 days or in the freezer for 2 weeks.

SWEET POTATO BROWNIES

🌙 Sound so wrong, but taste so good! 🌙

MAKES 8

1 ½ cups of mashed sweet potato

1 medium egg

1 cup of peanut butter, this can be substituted with almond butter or cashew butter

3 tbsp. of cacao powder

¼ cup of agave

2 tsp of ground cinnamon

1 tsp baking soda

It is best to prepare your sweet potatoes the night before and store in an airtight container in the fridge. To prepare the sweet potatoes bake in the oven at 180°c for 30 minutes or until soft inside. This will depend on the size of your sweet potatoes. Scoop out the soft centre when cool and mash.

Preheat oven to 180°c and line an 8 x 8 deep baking tray with baking paper and set aside for later.

Starting with the sweet potato and finishing with the egg, gently mix all ingredients into a large bowl and stir until well combined.

Pour the mixture into the baking tray

Bake in oven for 30 minutes. Your brownies should be firm on top but with a smooth middle.

How about serving your brownies with a peanut butter cream

Mix together ½ cup of Greek yogurt, ½ cup of peanut butter, tbsp. cinnamon and a tbsp. honey. Mix together and serve beside or on top of warm brownies.

OATY APPLE CRUMBLE WITH COCONUT ICE-CREAM

🌱 Why not try one of our alternative ice-cream flavours. 🌱

SERVES 4

8 large apples, peeled, cored and chopped

2 tbsp. cinnamon

1 tbsp. pure vanilla extract

2 cups Flahavan's Irish Porridge Oats

¼ cup butter

½ cup honey

½ cup pecans, finely chopped

FOR THE ICE-CREAM

2 cans unsweetened coconut milk

2 tbsp. vanilla extract with seeds

Preheat oven to 180°c

Brush a deep casserole dish, or individual smaller dishes with coconut oil

In a bowl mix together apples, 1 tbsp. of cinnamon and vanilla extract. Gently combine using your hands then transfer to your prepared dish.

In a separate bowl, combine honey, Flahavan's Irish Porridge Oats, butter, pecans and remaining cinnamon and spread this evenly on to the apple mixture.

Bake in preheated oven for 45 mins until golden brown and apples are soft.

FOR THE ICE-CREAM

Line a deep baking tray, 14 x 11inches, with baking paper and set aside.

Shake cans of coconut milk as if left sitting the contents can separate.

Pour coconut milk from the can into the tray and freeze for 3 to 4 hours.

Once frozen remove from tray and break into small chunks, add these to your food processor, add vanilla extract and blend until a thick texture is achieved.

Serve immediately with the warm apple crumble.

CHOCOLATE PEANUT BUTTER ICE-CREAM

SERVES 2

4 large bananas, quartered then frozen for 4 hours

1 tbsp. smooth peanut butter

2 tbsp. cacao powder

In a food processor, blend bananas until a smooth consistency is achieved. This may take some time as the banana may appear rough for a while but keep going remembering to stop occasionally to scrape the mixture off the sides.

Add in peanut butter to the banana mix and blend again.

Finally add in cacao powder and mix for a further 30 to 40 seconds.

Serve immediately. If you prefer a firmer ice cream return to the freezer for 20 minutes before serving.

STRAWBERRY BANANA ICE-CREAM

SERVES 2

4 large bananas, quartered then frozen for 4 hours

1 cup frozen strawberries

1 tbsp. vanilla essence

Follow the same method as above, bananas first, then strawberries and finishing with vanilla.

Again if you prefer a firmer ice cream, return to the freezer before serving.

This is not only a perfect quick dessert but a perfect post workout cooling treat – why not play around with flavours and try raspberries or some coconut!

LITTLE BIG PEOPLE

BAKED CHICKEN GOUJONS WITH SWEET POTATO WEDGES

We can't promise they will eat the veggies.

SERVES 2

CHICKEN GOUJONS

220g chicken breast, cut into thin strips

1 egg, beaten

½ cup almond meal

1 tbsp. garlic powder

pinch of salt and pepper

SWEET POTATO WEDGES

2 large sweet potatoes

2 tbsp. olive oil

pinch of salt and pepper.

CHICKEN GOUJONS

Preheat oven to 180°c and line a baking tray with baking paper.

Combine the almond meal, garlic and salt and pepper.

Lightly coat the chicken in the egg then cover in almond meal and seasoning. Repeat for all the chicken strips.

Place on the baking tray prepared earlier and bake for 30 minutes.

SWEET POTATO WEDGES

Preheat oven to 180 degrees and prepare a large baking tray with baking paper.

Cut the sweet potatoes in half, then half again. Then place in a large mixing bowl, add in the olive oil and seasoning and combine.

Bake for 30 minutes, then place under the grill for 3 to 4 minutes.

Serve immediately with the chicken goujons and a side of preferred vegetables.

LiTTLE CRiSPY QUiNOA BUNS

❧ Snap, crackle... and quinoa. ❧

4 cups quinoa pops

1 cup almond butter

1 cup agave

1 tbsp. vanilla essence

Preheat oven to 180°c and line an 8x8 baking tray with baking paper.

In a large saucepan over low heat mix together almond butter and agave until hot and runny. Do not let the mixture boil.

Remove from the heat and mix in the quinoa pops gently using a wooden spoon or spatula until all the mixture is combined.

Place the mixture in the prepared baking tray and press down evenly to roughly 1.5 inches.

Bake in the oven for 10 minutes to harden the top. Remove and set aside to cool before cutting into squares.

LiTTLE VEGETABLE SPiDERS

❧ A great way to disguise the greens. ☙

½ cup onion, finely diced

1 cup broccoli, finely chopped

½ cup courgette, grated

½ cup carrot, grated

1½ tbsp. arrowroot powder

2 eggs, whites only

2 tbsp. coconut oil

pinch salt and pepper

In a pan over low heat, gently soften onion and broccoli in coconut oil for 5 minutes.

In a large bowl combine the softened onion, broccoli, carrot and courgette.

In a separate bowl mix together the egg and arrowroot powder then add to the bowl with the mixed vegetables and thoroughly combine.

Spoon a small amount of mixture onto a pan over medium heat and gently cook until brown, turning regularly.
Do this with all of your mixture.

Serve immediately.

LITTLE FISH BITES

These were so easy to make we played with building blocks in between.

1 cup rice, cooked

½ cup carrot, sliced

½ cup broccoli, chopped

1 sea bass fillet,
bones removed.

Preheat oven to 200°c, when hot wrap the seabass in tinfoil and cook in the oven for 15 minutes. Remove and set aside to cool.

Fill a saucepan with water and bring to the boil over high heat, add carrots and broccoli and boil for 4 minutes until soft.

In a food processor, mix together the sea bass, carrot and broccoli to form a textured mix, you do not want this to be smooth.

In a bowl, gently combine the mixture with the cooked rice. Lifting out handfuls to shape into a ball by rolling between your palms.

Serve immediately.

RAWEOS

For copyright reasons we should point out these aren't KitKats.

¼ cup Linwoods
Milled Organic Flaxseed

¾ cup pecans

¼ cacao powder

1 cup medjool dates

1 tbsp. vanilla essence

FOR THE CREAM FILLING

¾ cup cashews soaked
overnight or in hot water
for 2 hours

2 tbsp. coconut oil

1 tbsp. agave

1 tbsp. vanilla essence

In a food processor mix together Linwoods Milled Organic
Flaxseed, pecans, cacao, dates and vanilla essence until a stick
consistency is formed.

Roll the mixture onto baking paper and flatten to 1cm thick.
Using a pastry cutter cut out 20 identical circles and place
in freezer.

Blend together cashews, coconut oil, agave and vanilla
until smooth.

Spread a teaspoon of the cashew mix onto a cookie
and top with another cookie.

Store in the fridge in an airtight container for up to 5 days.

LITTLE BROCCOLI CIRCLES

A great snack for after school until dinner time.

2 cups very finely chopped uncooked broccoli

¼ cup sweetcorn, chopped

½ cup mozzarella, grated

2 eggs, whites only

½ cup panko breadcrumbs

⅓ cup wholemeal breadcrumbs

pinch salt and pepper

Preheat the oven to 180°c and line a baking tray with baking paper or brush with coconut oil.

Place the chopped broccoli in a bowl of boiling water for 2 minutes, then remove and rinse with cold water.

In a large bowl mix together the broccoli, egg, sweetcorn, mozzarella, breadcrumbs and seasoning.

From the bowl take roughly a ¼ cup of the mixture and shape into a totty and place on the prepared baking tray.

Place in the oven and bake for 18 minutes, until golden brown and crispy, turning half way.

Serve immediately.

PEANUT BUTTER BANANZA ICE LOLLiES

🌰 There's nothing peanut butter can't fix. 🌰

2 medium bananas

½ cup smooth
peanut butter

1 tbsp. agave

1 tbsp. vanilla extract

½ cup almond milk

CHOCOLATE COATING

¼ cup melted coconut oil

¼ cup cacao powder

1 tbsp. agave

Dried fruits, desiccated
coconut and mixture
of nuts for decoration.
*optional

For this recipe you will need ice lolly moulds for 6 to 8 ice lollies.

Mix bananas, peanut butter, agave, vanilla and almond milk on a medium speed in a food processor until smooth.

Pour mixture into ice lolly moulds and leave to set in a freezer overnight.

When ice lollies are set and solid remove from freezer and moulds and lie flat on baking paper as you prepare the chocolate for coating.

In a bowl mix together melted coconut oil, cacao powder and agave.

Gently drizzle this chocolate mixture over the ice lollies and decorate with desired toppings. We prefer dried cranberries and coconut on some and chopped peanuts on others.

Return to the freezer for an hour to set the chocolate.

LiTTLE EGG MUFFiNS

How we like our eggs... in a muffin.

MAKES 10

You can choose a variety of fillings for your muffins but our personal favourites are spinach, cherry tomatoes halved, diced ham, bacon.

7 large eggs

¼ cup milk

½ cup mozzarella, grated

Salt and pepper *optional

Preheat oven to 180°c

For this recipe it is best to use silicone cupcake cases for easy removal.

Cook any of the fillings that require precooking, for example; sausage, bacon, chicken, and set aside.

In a medium bowl whisk together the chosen fillings, with the milk and eggs. You can also add some cheese to this mixture.

Set out the cupcake cases and distributive the mixture evenly between the cases. Filling roughly ¾ full allowing room for muffins to rise during cooking.

Sprinkle your remaining cheese on top of the mixture and bake in the oven for 30 minutes.

Once cooked thoroughly the muffins should feel firm. If they seem soft, return to the oven for a further 10-15 minutes.

Serve immediately.

LiTTLE FROYO FRUiTY BiTES

❡ Make these with the little ones or for the littler ones when teething. ❡

12 BITES

2 cups fat free Greek yogurt (plain or flavoured)

1 cup blueberries

1 cup strawberries, quartered

Lay out 12 silicone cupcake cases on a flat surface.

In a large bowl gently mix together yogurt, blueberries and strawberries.

Gently spoon out some of the mixture into each cupcake.

Place cases into the freezer for 2 to 3 hours or until solid.

Serve immediately.

Why not try some banana pieces or raspberries or even some chocolate chips.

THANK YOU

There are a number of people who came together to help
create this book and to the success of Slim's.

Kaizen Print for their creative input and design.

Mark Kelly at House of Fraser for letting us raid their homeware floor for
many of the plates, bowls and utensils you'll find in the photographs.

Sarah Shimmons at Linwoods for her support and enthusiasm
for this project and hopefully many more.

Flahavan's for helping us all start the day.

Khara Pringle for her endless energy and amusing us through
five twelve hour days shooting the photos.

My family for realising my potential and not admitting me
to a psychiatric hospital when the going gets tough.

All my staff for putting up with my mood swings
and believing in the Slim's ethos.

Rory Stuart for his daily pep talks and coffee.

Chris Love at Love PR for editing and overseeing this book
from beginning to end and for just being fabulous.

And to Kate Magill for all of the above and much, much more.

INDEX

INDEX